W9-ANP-635

DAKOTA

Big Buddy Books
An Imprint of Abdo Publishing
abdopublishing.com

Katie Lajiness

abdopublishing.com

Published by Abdo Publishing, a division of ABDO, PO Box 398166, Minneapolis, Minnesota 55439.
Copyright © 2019 by Abdo Consulting Group, Inc. International copyrights reserved in all countries. No part
of this book may be reproduced in any form without written permission from the publisher. Big Buddy Books™
is a trademark and logo of Abdo Publishing.

Printed in the United States of America, North Mankato, Minnesota.
052018
092018

THIS BOOK CONTAINS
RECYCLED MATERIALS

Cover Photo: Michael Matthews/Alamy Stock Photo.
Background Photo: Terryfic3D/Getty Images.
Interior Photos: Florilegius/Alamy Stock Photo (p. 30); Gary Warnimont/Alamy Stock Photo (p. 16); Getty Images
    (pp. 13, 15); INTERFOTO/Alamy Stock Photo (pp. 17, 21); Le Pictorium/Alamy Stock Photo (pp. 5, 19); Marilyn
    Angel Wynn/Native Stock (pp. 17, 23); North Wind Picture Archives (pp. 11, 25); Photo 12/Alamy Stock Photo
    (p. 26); robert cicchetti/Alamy Stock Photo (p. 9); VWPics/AP Images (p. 27); White House Photo/Alamy Stock
    Photo (p. 29); ZU_09/Getty Images (p. 17).

Coordinating Series Editor: Tamara L. Britton
Graphic Design: Jenny Christensen, Maria Hosley

Library of Congress Control Number: 2017962681

Publisher's Cataloging-in-Publication Data

Name: Lajiness, Katie, author.
Title: Dakota / by Katie Lajiness.
Description: Minneapolis, Minnesota : Abdo Publishing, 2019. | Series: Native Americans
    set 4 | Includes online resources and index.
Identifiers: ISBN 9781532115080 (lib.bdg.) | ISBN 9781532155802 (ebook)
Subjects: LCSH: Dakota Indians--Juvenile literature. | Indians of North America--Juvenile
    literature. | Indigenous peoples--Social life and customs--Juvenile literature. |
    Cultural anthropology--Juvenile literature.
Classification: DDC 970.00497--dc23

CONTENTS

Amazing People. 4

Dakota Territory 6

Home Life 8

What They Ate 10

Daily Life 12

Made by Hand 16

Spirit Life 18

Storytellers 20

Fighting for Land. 22

Back in Time 26

The Dakota Today. 28

Glossary 31

Online Resources 31

Index 32

Amazing People

Hundreds of years ago, North America was mostly wild, open land. Native American tribes lived on the land. Each had its own language and **customs**.

The Dakota (duh-KOH-tuh) are one Native American tribe. Many know them for their **ceremonies** and handmade crafts. Let's learn more about these Native Americans.

Did You Know?

The name *Dakota* means "ally."

Today, members of the Dakota tribe continue to teach their native customs.

Dakota Territory

The Dakota people are part of the Sioux (SOO) tribe. Long ago, the Sioux had many tribes. Today, there are three main tribes who speak different **dialects**. They are the Dakota, the Lakota, and the Nakota.

When the settlers moved to North America, the Dakota moved to the Midwest. They lived mostly in North Dakota, South Dakota, Minnesota, and Iowa.

CANADA

UNITED STATES

MEXICO

DAKOTA HOMELANDS

NORTH DAKOTA

MINNESOTA

WISCONSIN

SOUTH DAKOTA

NEBRASKA

IOWA

N
W · E
S

Home Life

The Dakota lived in teepees. Inside, people stayed warm in the winter and cool in the summer.

Teepees could be taken down and set up in a new place. Each teepee had 17 wooden poles. The poles were about 25 feet (8 m) long. The Dakota covered the teepees with buffalo hides.

A teepee's door always faced east so people could wake up with the sunrise.

What They Ate

Long ago, the Dakota ate corn, fruit, and potatoes. Later, horses made it easier to follow animal herds. So, buffalo, elk, and deer meat became a large part of their meals. Women cooked meat in pits or pounded it into a food called pemmican.

The Dakota dried meat to make jerky. This way, they had food throughout the winter.

Daily Life

The Dakota wore clothes made from animal skins. Everyone wore warm moccasins and animal hide robes. Men dressed in buckskin shirts, leather leggings, and loincloths. Women wore long dresses edged with fur.

The Dakota painted their bodies for ceremonies, dances, and war.

13

Within a Dakota tribe, men and women had different jobs. Everyone worked hard. Men hunted and fished. Women took care of the crops, made clothes, and set up teepees. Families tapped trees for sap they made into maple sugar. And, they grew corn, squash, and beans.

The Dakota gathered wild rice along bodies of water. They used cedar sticks to sweep the tall grasses into the boat.

Made by Hand

The Dakota made many objects by hand. They often used natural supplies. These arts and crafts added beauty to everyday life.

Mandan Bull Boat
A Mandan Bull Boat was made with one buffalo hide. The Dakota used it to float down the Missouri River.

Moccasins
Even babies wore beautifully beaded moccasins to keep their feet warm.

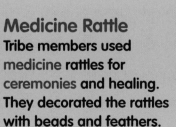

Painted Buffalo Hides
The Dakota painted hides to tell stories about their culture.

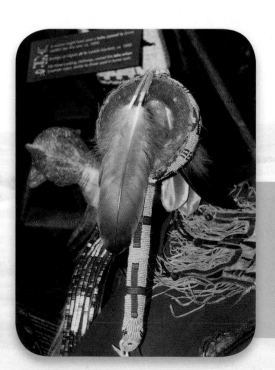

Medicine Rattle
Tribe members used medicine rattles for ceremonies and healing. They decorated the rattles with beads and feathers.

Spirit Life

Religion was a large part of native life. In the 1800s, the Dakota often practiced the Ghost Dance. People believed large buffalo herds would return. And, they thought past family members would come back to life.

However, the US government did not like the Ghost Dance gatherings. It forced tribes to stop this **tradition**.

The Dakota believed the Dog Dance gave them strength.

STORYTELLERS

Stories were important to the Dakota. The Dakota passed down their **religion** through storytelling. They told stories about forest spirits who lived in trees. These spirits were messengers who appeared to people in dreams.

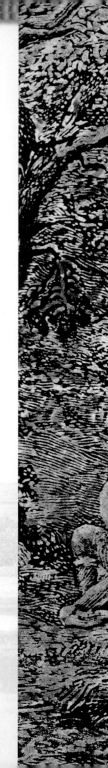

Tribe members gathered in the forest to hear stories. These stories helped them learn about their religion.

Fighting for Land

Upon meeting the Europeans, the Dakota had to give up their land. And they were required to change their **culture** and **traditions**.

The Dakota signed **treaties**, but new settlers still took over their lands. Then the government forced the Dakota onto **reservations**. And Dakota children had to go to **boarding schools**.

During the 1800s, religious teachers made the Dakota practice European religions.

    With little land for hunting, the government gave the Dakota cattle and corn. The tribe depended on the government. Yet there was still not enough food, so many people went hungry. When the Dakota fought back, the settlers burned their food and villages.

In the 1800s, railroad companies paid hunters to kill all the buffalo. With no food, the Dakota had to move onto reservations.

BACK IN TIME

1000

The Sioux lived near the Mississippi River. Each tribe was its own self-ruling village.

Mid-1600s

The Dakota had their first contact with Europeans.

1640s

Settlers on the East Coast forced the Dakota to move farther west into Minnesota.

1858

The **Treaty** of Washington gave nearly 12 million acres (5 million ha) of Sioux land to the United States.

1862

Angry about losing their land, Dakota men attacked new settlements in Minnesota. Later, the government ruled that 38 Dakota were to die for the attack.

1975

Congress passed laws allowing the Dakota to run their own schools. The Dakota had not done so since the 1880s.

1980

The government tried to pay $105 million to the Sioux in South Dakota. The tribes refused the money because they only wanted their old lands back.

2017

The Sioux stood up against the Dakota Access Pipeline. The pipeline would pump oil through the tribe's native lands.

THE DAKOTA TODAY

The Dakota have a long, rich history. Many remember them for their stories and their bravery in battle.

Dakota roots run deep. Today, the people have held on to those special things that make them Dakota. Even though times have changed, many people carry the **traditions**, stories, and memories of the past into the present.

Did You Know?

Today, there are about 4,000 Dakota people living in Minnesota.

Former President Barack Obama met Dakota people at the Cannon Ball Flag Day gathering in North Dakota.

"My white neighbors and friends know my character as a citizen and a man. I am at peace with every one."

— Chief Big Eagle, Dakota

GLOSSARY

boarding school a school at which most of the students live during the school year.

ceremony a formal event on a special occasion.

culture (KUHL-chuhr) the arts, beliefs, and ways of life of a group of people.

custom a practice that has been around a long time and is common to a group or a place.

dialect (dye-UH-lekt) a form of a language that is spoken in a certain region or by a certain group.

medicine (MEH-duh-suhn) an item used in or on the body to treat an illness, ease pain, or heal a wound.

religion the belief in and worship of God or gods.

reservation (reh-zuhr-VAY-shuhn) a piece of land set aside by the government for Native Americans to live on.

tradition (truh-DIH-shuhn) a belief, a custom, or a story handed down from older people to younger people.

treaty an agreement made between two or more groups.

INDEX

arts and crafts **4, 16, 17**

Chief Big Eagle **30**

clothes **12, 14, 17**

Dakota Access Pipeline **27**

fishing **14**

food **10, 11, 14, 15, 24, 25**

homelands **6, 7, 22, 24, 26, 27**

homes **8, 9, 14**

hunting **10, 14, 24, 25**

Lakota **6**

languages **4, 6**

Nakota **6**

North America **4, 6**

Obama, Barack **29**

religion **13, 17, 18, 19, 20, 21, 23**

reservation **22, 25**

Sioux **6, 26, 27**

stories **20, 21, 28**

travel **8, 10**

treaties **22, 26**

United States **6, 16, 18, 22, 24, 26, 27, 28, 29**